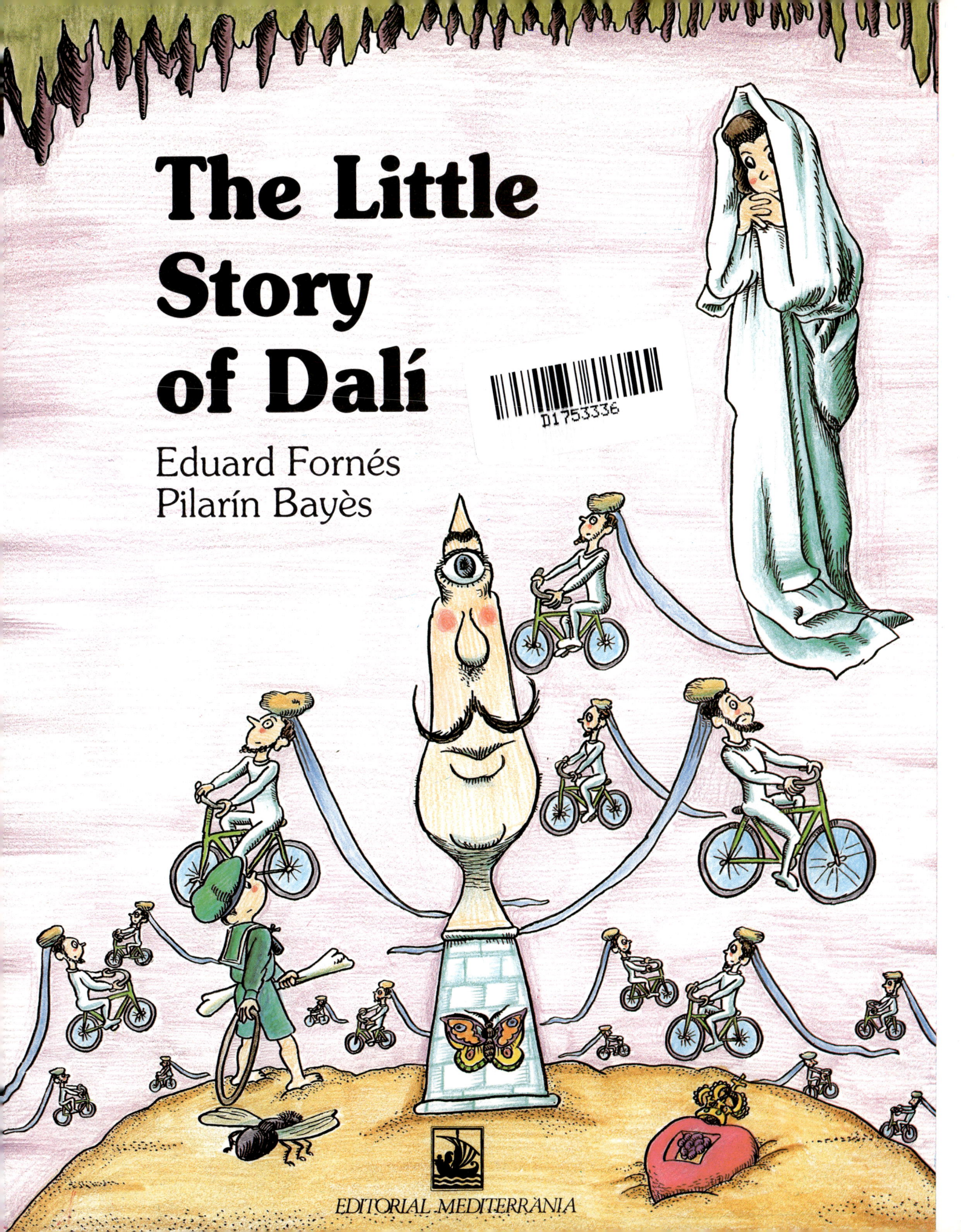

The Little Story of Dalí

Eduard Fornés
Pilarín Bayès

Childhood Memories

"On the 13th of May, 1904, Sr. Salvador Dalí i Cusí appeared in city hall in Figueres to register the birth of his infant son Salvador Felipe Jacinto, born on the 11th at 8:45 a.m. ....."

These are Dalí's own words taken from his delightful book, *The Secret Life of Salvador Dalí* by Salvador Dalí, where he concludes chapter three saying, "In one of the houses in Calle de Monturiol a new-born baby is being carefully and lovingly watched over by his parents, causing quite a commotion and no small fuss in the household. Alas! Remember what I am about to say, it won't be like that the day I die."

Dalí's father, a notary, was 41 when he was born; his mother was 30. Two years later his sister Ana María was born. He himself admits that his mother spoiled him to death. He was naughty and moody. In *The Secret Life* he tells about some of his pranks. He used to pull his sister's hair just to be mean and whenever his father punished him he would shout at the top of his voice and throw a temper tantrum until finally no one dared even scold him.

His life-long friend "Met" (Jaume Miravitlles) tells many funny stories about him. At school, he recalls Dalí making no effort at all as far as his studies were concerned. Arithmetic was beyond him. He would go home and back in his room he would start painting. His parents thought he was wasting his time.
In 1914, Dalí spent a few days at the home of the Pitxots in Cadaqués (the town where his father was from). He was greatly taken in by the Impressionist paintings he saw there.
In 1919, when he was 15, a monthly magazine called "Studium" came out in Figueres. Dalí began writing articles for it. He wrote about el Greco, Goya, Velázquez, Michelangelo, Dürer and Leonardo da Vinci.

In Search of Surrealism

One day Dalí's father was called to the bank where he was told someone had passed a false 25 peseta bill. Sr. Dalí asked his son whether he could tell which was the false bill. He instantly picked it out by some small variation in the drawing. His parents began to believe in his talent thanks to the insistance of his art teacher Sr. Núñez. Little by little they accepted the fact that he should study art at the School of Fine Arts in Madrid instead of law like his father.

In the fall of '21, Dalí went to Madrid to take the entrance exam. He was accepted but soon showed his nonconformity with the teaching methods used in the school. In his room he spent his time producing Cubist paintings. The following year he was expelled but he returned in 1924. It was then that he became closely acquainted with the poet García Lorca and the film-maker Luis Buñuel. Two years later, in 1926, García Lorca wrote his "Oda a Salvador Dalí". Buñuel filmed "Un chien andalou" in 1929 and after that the film that caused such an uproar in Paris: "L'âge d'or".

Just 21, Dalí had his first exhibition in the Dalmau Gallery in Barcelona. A newspaper of the day, La Publicitat, said, "Picasso and Miró take an interest in Dalí's work". The following year he went to Paris for the first time and met Picasso. On his return to Madrid for his final exams, he told his professors how incompetent they were and this time he was expelled for good. He then became the leader of the young nonconformists. The friendship between Lorca and Dalí brought Lorca to Cadaqués where they worked together on "Mariana Pineda" —Dalí doing the back-drops.

For three years Dalí wrote for L'Amic de les Arts, a magazine published in Sitges. During this time he published some 20 articles in which he expressed his doubts and his nonconformity to established art and culture. In March, 1929, Dalí, Lluís Muntanyà and Sebastià Gasch published their "Manifest Groc" (Yellow Manifesto) —a document written on yellow paper proclaiming their break with the culture of the age and the beginning of their struggle for a new culture. Later, in Paris, together with the group that made up the Surrealist Movement, they initiated the Surrealist Revolution.

On the 16th of October that year Dalí gave a lecture in the Parés Gallery in Barcelona entitled "Catalan Art: recent developments among young intellectuals". Opisso and Josep M.ª de Sucre, among others, took part in the discussion following. Dalí went so far as to say, "The time has come for us to shamelessly declare that we consider artistic endeavours and art in general to be nothing but loathsome rot totally useless to express present day feelings."

No other event caused so much ink to flow that year as that one did. Dalí had begun what was to be a constant in his life: provoking scandals and rejecting established art and culture. Moreover, his words were not always a true reflection or what he was actually thinking but or what he was searching for.

Gala's Dalí

At the age of 25 Dalí went to Paris for the second time. The "Manifest Groc" had already been published. Joan Miró met him at the station. He was introduced to René Magritte, André Breton and Camille Goemans who owned the art gallery where Dalí would have his first Paris exhibition at the end of the year. He then joined the Surrealist group. It was Goemans who introduced him to Paul Éluard. Éluard's wife's name was Gala. They had a daughter named Cecile. Gala, whose full name was Gala Dianaroff, was Russian by birth. She was a shy, restless person with a deep penetrating look.

Back in Cadaqués with his parents, Dalí invited his new friends to visit him. Buñuel and Magritte came and one day Paul Éluard and Gala also arrived by car. Dalí was busy painting that forceful, nearly terrorific picture called "Dismal Sport". In The Secret Life he tells about the visit and the fits of laughter he had during their stay laughing for hours on end and giving the impression of a madman.

Gala and Dalí became better acquainted. She sensed that he needed her. They fell in love. Éluard returned to Paris alone. Gala became the center of Dalí's visions and dreams. She was, as he put it, the incarnation of his way of thinking; the proof of the reality of that new analytic method he introduced into Surrealism under the name of the paranoiac-critical method. From then on Gala became the inspiration of his life and work —its central image. Those that have lived close to them are witnesses of the great love they felt for each other.

Surrealism Serves the Revolution

The 1930-31 season opened in Paris with the presentation, in Studio 28, of Buñuel and Dalí's film "L'âge d'or". An exhibition of Surrealist art accompanied the presentation. On December 3, members of the League of French Patriots interrupted the film and vandalized the hall and the paintings. The Prefecture of Paris initiated a campaign which brought about the banning of "L'âge d'or".

Ten days later, Dalí published the fundamentals of his paranoiac-critical method in "La femme visible". The following year he published "L'amour et la mémoire" (Paris, Éditions Surrealistes). In 1932 he published "Babaouo"; in 1935 "La conquête de l'irrationnel" in Paris and New York at the same time. Those were years full of activity for the Surrealist Movement. In 1933, Documents de Barcelona published Jaume Miravitlles' "El ritme de la revolució" illustrated by Dalí. Tension began to build up between Dalí and the other members of the Surrealist group. It reached its peak the following year. In February a meeting was called to oust Dalí. The order was signed by André Breton and Benjamin Péret, and in spite of Crevel,

Éluard and Tzara's opposition, Dalí was ousted. In October he had another show in the exhibition hall of the Llibreria Catalònia in Barcelona which concluded with a lecture by Dalí on "The Surrealist mystery and the phenomenon of the bedside table". To the fervour of Surrealism was added political turmoil. Dalí and Gala left for London. There they attended the opening of another exhibition. The following month they arrived in New York. Dalí called a press conference and showed up with a loaf of bread under his arm. He published a manifesto called "New York salutes me". A week later, he opened an exhibition in the Julien Levy Gallery. He presented the painting called "Gala with two grilled ribs on her shoulders" —a version of the William Tell myth in which Dalí exchanges the traditional apple for some appetizing ribs. It was during a lecture on the occasion that he pronounced his famous phrase: "The difference between me and a madman is that I am not mad."

At the time, Dalí was busy publishing articles in the different Surrealist magazines: La Révolution Surréaliste, Minotaure, Cahiers d'art, etc.

On his return to New York on the 7th of December, 1936, Time magazine dedicated the cover page to him. He had succeeded again!

The Salvador Dalí Myth

Exhibitions, lectures, articles and publications followed one after another, year after year.
In July, 1938, Dalí visited Sigmund Freud in London. The day after the visit Freud wrote a friend in Paris in these terms: The young Spaniard with the candid eyes of a fanatic and his undeniable masterly technique has made me reconsider my opinion of the surrealists.
The interpretation of Dalí's paintings and the study of his obsessions and myths help one understand what the painter is like.
When he was a little boy, according to what he tells us in The Secret Life, he was greatly impressed by a painting that hung in one of the halls at school: Millet's "Angelus". When he saw the painting again in 1929 he resolved to study it carefully. He even wrote an essay about its paranoiac-critical interpretation which he entitled "The tragic myth of the Angelus of Millet" but which remained unpublished until 1963. Upon Dalí's request, the Louvre museum X-rayed the painting and discovered a coffin with a dead child in it at the feet of the praying figures. The tragic myth Dalí had written about 23 years before had finally been brought to light.
All his life he searched for new forms with which to express a third dimension. This search brought him to meet with scientists and expound his theories to them. His deformed figures or anamorphosis produce a wonderful effect of rare perspective. The hologram registers the image through the light of a laser ray giving it a third dimension. His stereoscopic paintings produce an effect of total relief by means of superimposition of images. Among the best known are "Gala's Christ", "Dalí with his back to us painting Gala with her back to us", and "Dalí's hand drawing aside a golden veil in the shape of a cloud to discover Gala, the naked dawn, in the distance behind the sun."

On November 23, 1949, Pope Pius XII gave Dalí a private audience. The painter showed him the first draft of the "Madonna of Portlligat". This initiated a period in which religious themes predominate. He published his "Manifeste Mystique", painted his "Christ of Saint John of the Cross", "The temptations of Saint Anthony" and his "Last Supper". In 1951 and in 1954 he illustrated the Divine Comedy, the Bible and The Lord's Prayer. In 1957, before undergoing emergency surgery in New York, he called for a priest to administer to him the last rights. When he recovered he returned to Catalonia and married Gala on the 8th of August, 1958, in a church service in the church of Els Àngels in Girona.
The following year he visited Pope John XXIII and showed him the draft of a project to build a cathedral containing all the signs and symbols of Christianity.

Dalí was a genious. The marvellous light of the Empordà endowed him with great strength. His greatest works were produced in that paradisical setting of the sea of Portlligat and the rocks of Cadaqués. Using Portlligat as a starting point in his art, he discovers limitless horizons to us. This love for his homeland expresses itself in the union that exists in his landscapes. When after eight years, he returned to Europe and landed in El Havre, he went straight to Portlligat to feel at home again.

For fifty years (1930-1980) he worked almost non-stop. Before it is too late we want to acknowledge all those many hours there in his studio working away in silence creating a work that will immortalize him.

Dalí has had more that 150 private exhibits all over the world and has participated in some 200 collective shows, which means either a private or collective exhibition every other month throughout those 50 years. His written work is also very extensive. He has written more than 200 articles for magazines, besides books, poems, essays, etc. Up to 2,000 articles on his person and work have been catalogued. He has illustrated 102 books with drawings, water colours and lithographs; taken part in seven films and another seven have been made about him; designed the wardrobes and made the back-drops for plays such as García Lorca's "Mariana Pineda", William Shakespeare's "As you like it", the opera "Salomé", four ballets, etc. He has taken part in many radio programmes and television programmes and has made three records as well.

Dalí is a very cultivated person. His profound knowledge of art history makes him a real scholar for which he has been given awards all over the world. In May, 1979, he was invested honorable member of the Academy of Fine Arts of France. On the occasion, he gave a speech entitled "Gala, Velázquez et le Toison d'or".

His master pieces can be found in the most famous museums throughout the world. The Dalí Foundation, founded by his friend Reynolds Morse (first located in Cleveland, Ohio, but later moved to St. Petersburg, Florida) contains more than 200 of his most important paintings. There one can find "The Discovery of America", "The Ecumenical Council", "The Hallucinogenic Toreador", etc.

The Dali Theatre-Museum of Figueres

On the 28th of September 1974, at the age of seventy, Dali saw his greatest dream come true: the inauguration of the Dali Theatre-Museum in his own home town of Figueres. The whole town was one big celebration. People from everywhere turned out to give Dali an enthusiastic welcome. He arrived, accompanied by Gala, with the airs of an emperor under a brilliant display of fireworks and the pealing of church bells. Everyone hailed them. It was a day of real triumph for him.

During the Spanish Civil War a bomb had destroyed the roof of the Figueres Municipal Theatre. The building had remained in ruins and had served no useful purpose to the city until Dali decided to use the site for his museum. The restoration and adaptation of the theatre building to its new function were commissioned to the architects Ros and Bonaterra. Pérez Piñero designed the spectacular crystal dome which was to become the symbol of the city of Figueres. Dali also